BE THE
TOP **1**%
IN NETWORK MARKETING

7 Simple Steps to Leave the 99% Behind

KEITH & TOM "BIG AL" SCHREITER

Be the Top 1% in Network Marketing: 7 Simple Steps to Leave the 99% Behind

© 2022 by Keith & Tom "Big Al" Schreiter

Published by Fortune Network Publishing
PO Box 890084
Houston, TX 77289 USA
+1 (281) 280-9800

BigAlBooks.com
Print ISBN: 978-1-956171-10-5
Ebook ISBN: 978-1-956171-11-2

Contents

Preface.

I got this message. It said, "I'm going to be in the top 1% and make a lot of money in network marketing because I am hungry to succeed."

Uh … news flash.

There are millions of network marketers right now who are "hungry to succeed." If you are the person who wrote that message, bad news. You are not unique. It's going to take a lot more than wanting and wishing. We have to beat out the other 99% who also want to succeed.

Now, "wanting to succeed" is important. It is step #2 in our plan. But we have to do a lot more than step #2 if we are going to be in the top 1%.

Is it complicated? No.

Is it hard? No, not exceptionally hard. But it will take consistent work to make sure we cover the other steps to get to the top 1%.

If it isn't hard, and it only takes some easy-to-learn consistent steps, then why don't more people take the steps?

Because they don't even know there are steps. Instead, they try random things that don't work. They take advice from 100 different gurus with 100 different plans, all leading in different directions. And then it gets worse. They are not sure that their plans will work out. It is hard to feel long-term motivation when they are unsure if they will get the results.

Let's make this simpler.

Want to be in the top 1% in our network marketing business?

Ask ourselves this question, "Why don't 99% make it to the top?"

The answer is obvious. The 99% did something different than the 1% that made it to the top.

We have to do the things that 99% of people are not willing to do. Let's take a quick look at the 7 steps that will help us get there:

Step #1. Show up. This seems like a no-brainer, but we are surprised how many people give up before they even get started. If we want to be successful, we have to show up every day and take consistent action.

Step #2. We must have an emotional reason to build our network marketing business. Our why has to be big enough to keep us motivated through the tough times. It's not enough to want to make more money. We have to be passionate about our business and believe in what we are doing.

Step #3. Personal development. Growth mindset. If we want to be successful, we have to keep learning and growing. We need to develop a growth mindset and be open to new ideas.

Step #4. Learn network marketing skills. We can't be successful in our business if we don't have the right skills. We need to learn how to prospect, how to sell, how to follow up, and how to build relationships.

Step #5. Get hands-on experience in our new skills. Once we've learned the skills, we need to get out there and start using them. We need to get comfortable with how our prospects react and learn from our mistakes.

Step #6. Teach our professional networking skills to others. Once we've mastered the skills, we need to help others do the same. We can do this by sharing our knowledge with others and helping them to grow their businesses.

Step #7. Making success automatic. The final step is to make our success automatic. This means we need to have systems and activities in place that will help us to achieve our goals. We need to have a plan and be organized, so that we can focus on the things that are important to us.

Now, let's get to work and learn how to fill in the blanks so that we can be in the top 1% in our network marketing business.

Most of the bad experiences in this book are mine. And all the good advice is Keith's.

Thanks for reading!

—Keith & Tom

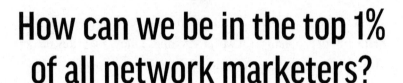

How can we be in the top 1% of all network marketers?

Easy!!!

- Be the only child of the president or prime minister of our country.
- Be a famous movie star with a billion social media followers.
- Be a world-famous athlete that people adore. Yes, people will flock to join our team.

Now, if we are one of these people, we're probably not reading this book. We are sitting by the pool in our Tahitian mansion, sipping tropical drinks, and having the vice-president of our servant staff read this book to us.

Well, if we are not one of these "special" lucky people, then what? What if we were not born with a silver spoon in our mouths? What if we are not rich, famous, or influential? Do we have a chance?

What about us who are not "thick-skinned" or obsessively motivated? Is success possible for us? Do we have a chance?

Yes. Not only do we have a chance, but a very good chance. In fact ...

Getting to the top 1% isn't that hard.

Why?

Because few people even try. Our competition gave up at the first whiff of problems. All we have to do is follow a few key principles. Then, we too can enjoy the open view from the top.

Forget lottery ticket mindset. Forget hoping and wishing. Stop sitting in front of vision boards.

Instead, let's follow these 7 basic steps to the top.

7 steps?

That doesn't sound that complicated, does it? But we may be asking ourselves, "So why don't more networkers follow these steps?"

The answer?

If they don't know what these basic 7 steps are, then how can they do these steps? They get frustrated because they don't know what works and doesn't work, what they are missing, and how to fix their progress. They stop growing.

We won't have that problem. We will use these 7 basic steps as a compass to point us in the right direction, directly to the top 1%.

So let's take a trip to the top and make our success happen.

Ready for Step #1? Let's go!

STEP #1:
Show up!

Show up? That's it? Really?

Uh … no. But showing up is a great start.

Showing up is not the only thing, but it is a requirement. There is an old saying, "Quitting reduces our chances for success by over 50%!"

Yes, many people begin and then quit within days of starting. Definitely hurts their odds of success. It is like dieting. Quitting early doesn't work.

When I joined network marketing, I was ultra-naive. I didn't know you could quit. I had never been in business, or even studied a single business course. They told me to sign up, and then go to work. Made sense to me. Was I terrified of failing? No. They didn't mention failing at the opportunity meeting, so I never thought of that option.

I just … showed up.

Meetings, trainings, rallies … I was there. Usually sitting alone in the back row.

What about others who joined when I started? Most disappeared in weeks. It is hard to fail if we don't quit. Showing up gives us a chance.

Everyone can show up, but not everyone will.

Here is proof!

In 5th grade, I was the #1 student in my class. I rocked!

It was easy.

All I had to do was to … show up!

I went to a one-room rural schoolhouse in Nebraska. No running water. All nine grades are in one room with a teacher with uh … limited credentials. The school was basic.

But … 6th grade was different. I got a classmate named, Lena. While I am still socially awkward now, I was worse in 6th grade. We didn't talk. So I was #2 in my class until halfway through the year when she and her family moved to a different farm and school. Yeah! I was back at the top of my class.

And all I did was show up. Sometimes persistence is better than talent.

We fail a lot before we succeed.

Babies got it right. When learning to crawl and walk, they fail 100% of the time until finally, they succeed.

Do they give up and quit while they are in the failing part of their journey? Do they tell themselves this? "I don't know how to do this. It hurts when I fall. I can't make this work. Forget it. This is embarrassing. I will lay here as a baby blob."

Nope. Babies show up every day until one day, they figure it out. They don't give up even though they experience 100% failure for several months. That is harsh! What keeps them going?

Babies see other people crawl, stand and walk. They know it is possible, but they don't know how to do it ... yet! They don't make a final judgment on their current results.

When we start our business, it is the same for us. We know success is possible. We see others enjoying their careers. While we don't know the missing pieces yet, we do know that we can learn what we don't know yet.

We are only one person away from changing our lives.

The good news is that we don't need to have a superstar transformation. Here is what is possible.

Out of nowhere, months from now, we talk to someone, who talks to someone, who talks to someone ... who joins our business and creates a tsunami wave. All of a sudden, we are on our way. One person. Just one person can make all the difference in the world.

Want to have nightmares? Consider this.

What if we stopped? No longer showed up? And that one person never learns about our business. Not only would that person's life suffer, but what about us? We missed the opportunity to transform our life, because we didn't show up.

Persistence rocks. We have to stay in the game to win.

Why do people give up so fast?

Because the human mind loves to work in the now. The human mind thinks in the now. Now is powerful. The future? Well, we discount the future. Does this sound familiar?

We are watching an engaging late-night television show. Logically, we tell ourselves, "I should go to bed now. I have to wake up early for work."

Our emotional brain laughs and takes control, "Ah, this show is so good. Worry about feeling tired tomorrow. Let's watch another hour longer."

Or, we are at a party and enjoying deep-fried, bacon-wrapped candy bars. Our logical brain says, "Don't even consider it."

Our emotional brain feels no guilt as we stuff down two more of these delicious treats, and tells us, "Maybe I should have one more. I will exercise tomorrow."

We know how this ends. We stay up late and feel exhausted at work the next day. We hate ourselves for eating too much, again.

Why is our human brain so weak?

Because we live in the now. The future is unsure. We don't feel we have control. We can't feel success is imminent. So what do we do?

We stop thinking and live in the now. And we don't move forward to the future we desire.

To succeed in network marketing, we have to take daily action steps that move us closer to our goal. We call these baby steps. And as long as we are taking steps, even tiny baby steps, in the right direction, we eventually get to the top 1%.

Nice.

When we take our baby steps, our mind relaxes. We don't have to be perfect. We don't have to be an expert today. We don't have to accomplish everything this week. The key is to know that every moment, we make progress.

The secret is that everything we do moves us a little closer. We are going in the right direction. That feels good to our "now" brain.

Baby steps?

As we are reading this book now, we are taking our first baby step already! Step #1 is to show up. If we make mistakes along the way, welcome to normal! Further proof we are human. Even if we sit in the back row, we are still showing up. Even if we don't have a guest or prospect, we are still showing up.

This is a baby step. No need to overcomplicate. We can do this.

So don't I have to take impulsive, over-the-top, massive action immediately?

Not really. Massive action can be very good, if we know what we are doing.

Taking massive action in the wrong direction puts us further from our vision to be in the top 1%. Consider the difference between:

- Massive action.
- Consistent action.
- Effective action.

Which one is best? Effective action, of course. We want results.

Next best? Consistent action. With consistent action, we gradually move forward, hopefully in the right direction.

And finally, massive action. Massive action is great, but only if we are doing the right thing.

Whoa! Whoa! But wait …

Let's not under-react and go into inactivity mode.

This doesn't mean we should wait and avoid action. Only a warning that it might be good to get a tip or two to make our early people encounters more effective and less cringy. A few smart tips could save us a lot of time and misery. No use wasting time and effort doing stupid things that get us 100% failure.

So let's not use learning as an excuse to avoid action. We can do both at the same time. We don't want to be those professional students who attend trainings 100% of their time, just so they can avoid having to talk to people.

So, what are the odds we know exactly what to say and do when we start?

Not good. I said the worst things when I started. I didn't burn my bridges. I nuked them! Yes, I took massive action, but it was the wrong type of action.

It makes sense to get a few words of advice and direction when we start. We don't have to be an expert, but let's not ruin our chances either.

Some examples of massive action without advice?

1. Bomb demolition. I would ask advice about which wire to cut before I took massive action. A quick lesson could save our lives.

2. Flying an airplane. I went to ground school and took an instructor with me for my first few flights. If we don't read a book or get some instruction, yes, we could fly our first time, but it may be our last time.

3. Surgery. I hope my surgeon reads a how-to guide before cutting. Same with the anesthesiologist.

4. Rushing from the opportunity meeting, stopping random prospects and saying, "You have a terrible job. Don't be stupid. Join my opportunity." Uh … just speaking from personal experience here.

Yes. Take action, but make sure it is effective action.

We don't have to know everything when we start. A little bit will do. How about an easy shortcut to some best practices?

That is why we have a sponsor. And we have books, audios, guides, and common sense. If we want to reach the top 1%, let's at least put our effort in the right direction.

If we are clueless, here is the good news. We keep showing up. We learn. And we get better. It is hard to fail if we never quit.

It is us vs. the demons in our heads.

"I don't know if this is for me."

Whoops! The networker said this too loudly. The lights flicker … and his personal magic genie appears.

Genie: "I heard your stress. So sorry to hear you are discouraged and not growing in your business."

Networker: "I don't need you to tell me that. I know I am stuck. Use your magic powers! Fix this for me!"

Genie: "Uh … there are rules for magic genies. We can only do magic to fix the stuff you can't do. I can't do everything for you. Change your own diapers. Put on your big boy's pants. You can grow your business if you want."

Networker: "Easy for you to say. You are not out there getting rejected. You don't have friends hoping you fail. You don't have to worry about inflation or a dream-sucking vampire boss."

Genie: "So what have you tried to do to fix this so far?"

Networker: "I tried everything I know. I can't think of anything new that will work."

Genie: "Got it. You are so right. You are not going to grow your business. Doing only what you know now … will keep you where you are now. So how does it feel to be stuck?"

Networker: "Fix it! Fix it! I don't want to stay stuck!"

Genie: "Sorry. Genie rules. Remember? We are not allowed to fix things you can do yourself. So why not stay where you are? Mediocrity isn't so bad. Lots of your friends do it. Give up on your dreams and enjoy some donuts on your slow and steady progression to death."

Networker: "Ha, ha. Shut up! I don't want lectures. If I don't know what to do to grow faster, then I am stuck here forever?"

Genie: "Yes. Enjoy. Mediocrity looks good on you."

Networker: "G-r-r-r. Talk to my hand. Lazy magic genies don't have to worry about this stuff. But, I won't sit, dream about magic, and quit. I will take action to learn what I don't know. I won't stay stuck where I am. I will grow! Tomorrow is another chance to learn and move forward."

Genie: "Are you sure? Won't you talk yourself out of it? Don't you think it would be easier to give up now and just hate your life as it is? Hey, I heard there are some funny cat videos on the Internet. Did I tell you procrastination is a virtue? Why not listen to your friends who want you to fail? They are your friends, right? You know, credit card debt looks good on you. Hey, want to buy a lottery ticket?"

Networker: "Nice try. You know, you are sort of a loser genie. Not very good at your job. Go ahead. Sit on your butt. I can do this without you! I am not giving up and quitting because of an imaginary, incompetent genie inside of my head."

Baby steps.

Sometimes our biggest obstacle is our minds. We can defeat this formidable opponent. How?

Just keep showing up.

Quitting is easy. We quit jobs. We quit diets. We quit watching television at night so that we can wake up in the morning. Quitting feels natural for us as humans because we do it so often.

But if we are going to be in the top 1%, we can't quit and restart every three months. All companies have problems. If we give up on the first obstacle to try something different, this will be our pattern forever.

Look at the 1% at the top. They are not there because they didn't have challenges or obstacles. They are at the top because they overcame these challenges and obstacles. Problems will happen. Don't stress. Problems are only mild speed bumps along our journey.

The reward for people who show up?

Every new day brings a new opportunity for breakthroughs.

STEP #2:
Our emotional reason to succeed in our business.

If we don't have a strong emotional drive, we will run out of gas, quit at the first whiff of resistance, and give up on our business dreams.

Our logical brain can rationalize anything, including quitting. But if we have a big emotional reason to succeed, we will ignore the obstacles and push through while our competition gives up on their dreams.

Our brains work like this.

We make decisions based on emotion, not logic. After we make our emotional decision, our brains make up some logical reasons that sound good. We want these logical reasons to justify our actions to our spouse or friends. But make no mistake, emotion rules.

And what about taking action?

Action comes from emotion, not logic. We can't logic ourselves or our prospects into action. Logic may have impressive reasons, but few people will join a march on their country's capital based on a PowerPoint presentation.

Emotion rules.

If logic alone were enough, nobody would smoke cigarettes or speed while driving. Everyone would exercise and eat right every day and donuts wouldn't exist. Our customers would buy our products and ignore our competitors. Our team would embrace every change we make, and our kids would do everything we say.

Yeah, right! Reality proves that logic is not enough to get us to do what we need to do.

What are some emotional reasons to start our own business?

- To have a better life for our family.
- To spend more time with family.
- To quit a boring job.
- Because we hate our boss.
- For more money.
- To make a difference in the world.
- We don't get enough vacation time on our job.
- We want to do something more exciting and fulfilling.

These are all valid reasons, but are they strong enough to keep us going when the going gets tough? Could we make these reasons emotionally stronger? How about these?

- We want to prove to ourselves that we can do it. Some of us thrive on challenges. We enjoy pushing our personal limits higher and higher.
- We want to show our family and friends that we're not failures. Maybe our classmates voted us to be "least likely to succeed" in our high school class. Or, we want to prove our in-laws wrong by showing them we are not the loser

they think we are. Or, we want to earn more than our worthless brother-in-law who makes fun of our car.

- We want to make a difference in the world by solving problems that we're passionate about. We want to give more to our preferred charitable causes. We feel a strong and rewarding purpose in life by helping humanity move forward.

- We didn't get the education we wanted when we were young. Now is our chance to earn enough money to send our daughter to that fancy private school.

- We want the freedom to travel and experience the world. Why should we watch other people's experiences on a television travel channel when we could be living the experience?

- We hate being treated like a six-year-old child. It is humiliating to ask permission for toilet breaks or having a supervisor telling us our break time is over. After all, what is wrong with taking back-to-back breaks? Or triple servings of coffee? We only live once.

- Our biological clock programmed us to be an "evening" person. We have a hate relationship with our morning alarm. We want to stop the daily aggravation of the morning alarm. We desire to wake up only when we are tired of sleeping.

What is the emotional reason that will keep us going when the going gets tough? What is our big emotional reason to succeed in our business?

When we have an emotional reason, that becomes an obsession. It will remind our minds to look for reasons why we should continue. This helps our minds to suppress our default wiring to take the easy road and quit.

Instead of constantly pushing ourselves, let's make this more fun with a strong emotional reason to succeed in our business.

Does emotion make that much difference? Are we sure logic is overrated?

When we're unhappy in our job, it can be tough to stay motivated. We may feel like we're stuck in a rut and that our career is going nowhere. But logically, we tell ourselves to grind out the day for a paycheck. That is a tough way to start the day, every day.

Unfortunately, if we don't have a strong motivational reason to take action, we will default to living this same experience, over and over again, until ... well, we know how this sentence ends.

Logic talks, but our brains ignore the message.

Irritating friend: "Want to stop watching television and take a walk?"

Me: "No, I am fine. I'll sit here and protect my body joints from wear and tear."

Irritating friend: "A little exercise is good for you. Plus, you need to get out and get a bit of fresh air. Your Food Channel binge-watching is an addiction."

Me: "I am improving my mind one recipe at a time."

Irritating friend: "You know, they just opened a new donut shop at the end of the block ..."

Whoooossshh! A blur crosses the room.

Me: "What is taking you so long? I can only hold this door open for you for so long. Come on. Let's go!"

Our logic tells, "No donuts. Too much sugar, unhealthy synthetic flavors, additives, preservatives, and trans fats. A culinary disaster."

But our brains ignore our well-crafted logic. What is our brains' reply?

"Release the emotions! Activate the feel-good serotonin, dopamine, endorphins, and oxytocin hormones! Incoming donuts! Prepare to overeat. Run, don't walk to the new donut shop!"

Instant action.

This is why we need to put our emotions to work for us, instead of against us. The more powerful the emotion, the easier it will be for us to take action when we face challenges.

Need another food example of how emotions override logic?

We see two storefronts.

Storefront #1: "The Sweaty Gym Torture Experience." Hmmm. We ask ourselves, "Should I go home, put on workout clothes, come back and exercise to burn a few hundred calories?"

Storefront #2: "Grand Opening Grand Buffet! All-you-can-eat." Hmmm. We think, "Yeah, better go here instead. Quicker and more convenient."

And we can justify our decision with logic.

- I will save the environment by not driving home and back.
- I don't want to take up space in the gym in case someone needs it more than me.
- I will only eat healthy at this buffet.
- I should support new businesses.

- I could injure myself in the gym.
- And …

Okay, the logic list is endless.

Here is the final score:

Emotion: 1

Logic: 0

So how can I find my core emotional reason to build my business?

Start by choosing which of these core values will motivate us. Here is a list from our book, "Motivation. Action. Results." Ready?

1. Power.
2. Financial security.
3. Desire to be rich.
4. Desire to look good.
5. Loving relationship with a partner.
6. Family.
7. Career fulfillment.
8. Desire to feel needed.
9. Personal enlightenment.
10. Adventure/travel/adrenaline junkie.
11. Aim for fame.
12. Popularity.
13. Accomplishments.
14. Desire to have a good time.

Let's imagine this core value makes us excited, #11 - Aim for fame. We dreamed our entire life to be someone people would notice. We smile when we dream about getting an award on stage.

This emotion drives us to stretch out of our comfort zones. We have the urge to create something awesome. We want to do something now to advance us toward our goals.

Now, let's imagine we have core value #6 - Family. We think about our loved ones and how we want to make our lives better together. We have a deep emotional connection to this feeling. This inspires us to work hard so we can enjoy even better times together.

These are two examples, but we get the idea. Emotions drive action.

When we have a strong emotional reason, moving from inaction to action is easy. We can't wait to move closer to our values and goals.

If our emotional reason is strong, we know it already!

Yes, we won't even have to think about these 14 core values and which ones apply to us. We know exactly what got us excited when we joined our business.

But, if we don't have a strong emotional reason ... uh-oh. Did we pick our business logically, and have no passion for our outcome? If we did, then we sentenced ourselves to a lifetime of pushing ourselves instead of wanting to move forward. This gets tedious and we will tire quickly. Plus, every obstacle will appear as a career-shattering villain. Quitting becomes easy.

Stop now.

If we don't have our emotional reason yet, then stop where we are.

Try to see a future vision of where we want to be. What will that look like? And more importantly, how will that feel?

Getting this emotional reason is the fuel that will motivate us forward for the rest of our careers. Let's not start our journey with an empty gas tank.

So having my "emotional reason" is more important than everything else?

It is one part of our success. It is hard to say that one part of a car is more important than the other. Is the engine of our car more important than the wheels? Is our brain more important than our heart? We will need both.

Of course we need to learn skills to build our business. But will we have motivation to learn new skills without an emotional reason to invest that learning time?

Take a moment to write down our emotional reason on some yellow sticky notes. Place our notes in visually conspicuous places so that we have a reminder of what inspires us to take the next step.

We need motivation and inspiration to fuel our journey.

STEP #3:
Personal development.

Carol Dweck popularized the term, "growth mindset." What is a growth mindset?

People with a growth mindset believe their abilities can be developed through:

- practice
- hard work
- perseverance.

Growth mindset people are more open to learning new things and attempting challenging tasks.

What is the opposite of a growth mindset?

A fixed mindset. People who believe they are stuck with what abilities they currently have. They don't want to attempt learning new things because they feel it won't make a difference. They feel resigned to where they are.

How about an example?

A fixed mindset would say: "I'm not good at math."

A growth mindset would say: "I need to invest extra effort to improve my math skills, but I can learn to get better."

We hear prospects with fixed mindsets tell us these objections:

- I am not good at business.
- I could never learn to do that.
- This sounds too hard to do.
- I am not good at selling.
- Why try? I will only fail.
- This will take too long.
- I tried and failed with something like this before.
- I don't have any energy.
- I don't have any time.
- I don't have any money.
- I don't know enough.
- It's not worth it.
- I wouldn't know where to start.
- I don't know any people.
- I am too shy to leave my room.
- Nothing ever works for me.
- I would love to go the extra mile, but there might be a lot of traffic there. I better stay where I am.

The above objections arise from fixed mindsets. These prospects decided they can't do something without even trying. They gave up before they started! We can feel the resignation in their voices. Frustrating and sad to watch.

Now as we look at these objections, we think, "I don't want to sound like that. I don't want to give up before I even had a chance to try. I want a growth mindset!"

Good choice.

If we are reading this book now, we have a growth mindset. Great news for us.

Knowing our destination gives us a direction.

We want to be in the top 1% in network marketing. Without a goal, it is impossible to know which direction to start our journey.

Think about people without goals. Motivation is hard. They tend to drift in the easiest direction. Their Maslow's Pyramid looks something like this.

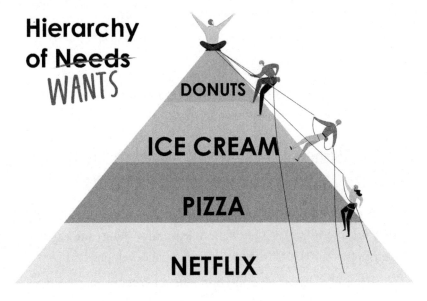

Let's choose a good direction if we want to put effort into our lives. We want to look back and proudly say, "I spent my time wisely."

Zig Ziglar said, "If you don't know where you're going, you'll probably end up somewhere else."

Goals make sure we put our efforts in the right direction. Since we are reading this book, we know our goal already, to be in the top 1% in network marketing. We are moving in the right direction.

Goals help us answer questions like these.

- Where do we want to be in five years?
- What do we want our lives to look like?
- How do we want to feel as we live our lives?
- How much money do we want to earn?
- How much time and freedom do we desire?
- What kind of lifestyle do we want to live?
- Do we want our efforts to make a difference to others?
- Who do we want to help?

If we don't answer these questions for our lives, then someone else will answer these questions for us. Ouch.

So how does our growth mindset relate to personal development?

People with a growth mindset continually work on themselves. They want to improve. They want to learn new things and expand their potential. This is what we call personal development.

We make deliberate and conscious choices to improve ourselves in some way. We can choose to improve our:

- Attitude.
- Skills
- Character.
- Knowledge.

- Mindset.
- Abilities.
- Health.
- Relationships.

Plenty of areas for us to choose.

Remember those fixed mindset people? They would say, "I don't need personal development. I am good enough." But that is them talking, not us.

Personal development takes us from where we are now, to where we want to be in the future.

If we believe in constant improvement, then our personal growth will never stop. No finish line for us here. We want our lives to be better.

Personal growth is a journey, something we live every day. It is not a destination. It is not someplace we get to … and then stop.

So where do we start?

Here is the secret that explains everything.

"The only thing between us, and where we want to be, is a whole bunch of things that we don't know … yet."

If we already knew these things, then we would already be where we wanted to be!

This is where a growth mindset helps. We know we have to learn more, and we believe that we can. People with fixed mindsets give up at this point.

But, here is the challenge.

We don't know what we don't know. And if we don't know what we don't know, then how will we ever figure out what we don't know? How can we learn new things when we don't know what to learn?

Thankfully, there is a solution.

We have books, audio instruction, mentors, seminars, workshops, and a world of information and skills from people who have gone before us. This is where we will find the answers to our question, "What do I have to learn to go to the next step?"

Where is the best place to start?

Everyone has a different starting point. Do some people have a head start? Yes, and that is okay. We need to start building from where we are now.

Don't worry about that superstar on stage. Don't worry about that person with the magic personality. Don't worry if some people seem to have natural advantages.

It doesn't matter where we start, as long as we point in the right direction. That means every little thing that we learn, moves us closer to where we want to be. Our progress accumulates. We get better every day like a giant snowball rolling down a hill.

Management expert, Peter Drucker, said, "The best way to predict your future is to create it."

Where did I start?

Near the bottom. Okay, maybe I had to look up just to see the bottom. It wasn't pretty.

When I started, I was a shy, nerdy, personality-free, charisma-bypassed, socially awkward wallflower, and should not have been allowed out in public. Not a pretty site. My childhood was on a remote rural farm, and all I had to talk to were the cows. Later, I studied engineering. Engineering students don't even talk to each other. If there was an award for invisible, or least-remembered, I would have made the hall of fame. I was ill-prepared to start even basic conversations. A conversation with a stranger was terrifying. I didn't even have the advantage of being a social media influencer. Oh, and I wasn't an Instagram model.

Did I have a lot to learn? Oh my. I had to learn almost everything from scratch. I was even clueless about basic social manners. I had never heard the words "goal-setting" in school. Everything I learned was a new discovery.

I started with an audio. No, I didn't download this audio from an imaginary Internet. It wasn't on a CD. On audio cassette tape? No, they hadn't been invented yet. It was on a scratched, vinyl, 45 rpm record. My sponsor loaned me this single recording from Earl Nightingale called "The Strangest Secret."

Did I grasp the message? No. I was clueless. But, it did give me a hint that there was a lot that I didn't know. I was pointed in the right direction.

The journey ahead

This is a long road. There is no end destination. Our goalposts will always move as we get better. That is good news. Our personal growth should never end. We can always improve. Life is our adventure. Let's experience life at a higher level.

Education is expensive.

Not in money, but in time. When I started in network marketing, I didn't have a budget for self-improvement. Where could I go to learn more?

The obvious source of great ideas and information is from books. Thank goodness for a free library system. It didn't take long to go through their limited selection of self-improvement books, but by that time I already knew exactly what I wanted to learn.

Next step? Search some used bookstores. There was not much available 50 years ago, but another baby step.

Today? Many successful people have made their network marketing journey before us. Let's learn some of their lessons to speed up our growth.

What are the first lessons I learned in my personal development journey?

Attitude.

I never knew there was such a thing. But, I learned that attitude was the lens through which I saw the world, and how the world saw me. Did I have a bad attitude before? Maybe not a horrible attitude, but certainly I was a self-appointed skeptic of everything. Few people want a skeptical friend or a skeptical business associate.

I worked on having a more positive and supportive point of view, and guess what? More positive reactions happened immediately.

Instead of criticizing other people's ideas, I tried to be more supportive. More people would stay in conversation with me. Huge progress for this introvert. My family noticed and appreciated my improved attitude also. I was on my way!

Goals.

I spent my entire life as a follower trying to fit in. I accepted what other people told me to do. It never occurred to me to have an original plan. Did I know how to set smart goals, better goals, or actionable goals? No. That would come later.

There is an old saying, "If we don't know where we are going, then any road will take us there." That was how I lived my life, without a clue and without direction. Baby steps.

Relationships.

I thought relationships happened automatically, but I learned that we could create them. We don't have to passively hope someone will like us or connect with us. We can take the initiative to get to know others better and make new friends.

Action.

I read successful people took action. Everyone has ideas. Nothing special in having ideas. But, successful people put ideas into motion and get results. That made sense to me, so I took action on every idea that crossed my path. Some ideas worked, and some didn't. That was okay. I knew that if I kept taking action, something would work for me.

Procrastination.

I was good at procrastination. But, this is not a good habit to master. Was I lazy? That could be true. I thought, "Why get motivated when I don't know what I want?" Having a goal helped me have a reason to start taking action. I was beginning to see where all these personal development skills were coming together. There is power in synergy.

Reactions.

Whew! This was a big revelation to me.

Most humans go through life on autopilot, reacting to whatever happens to them at the moment. If we smile at them, they smile back. If we say "hi" to them, they say "hi" back to us. What happens when we go into a retail store? What do we say when the sales clerk asks us, "Can I help you?" What is our automatic reply? "Oh no, I am just looking."

What if I changed my reply to, "Yes, I am looking for a gift for my sister's birthday." Whoa! A totally different reaction from the sales clerk. I learned that I could affect the reactions of others by changing my word. Oh my!

Do we see a pattern yet?

These responses are examples of automatic programs in our human brains. These programs control our behaviors automatically, without thinking about them. And these automatic reactions are powerful.

Humans go through life reacting, reacting, and reacting.

Now, here is the question.

We meet a prospect. Does the prospect's behavior have anything to do with the prospect? Or does our prospect's behavior have everything to do with what we say and what we do?

This was a tough lesson for me to learn.

I realized that I wasn't a victim of the current circumstances, but that I caused these circumstances.

If people are reactive, and they react negatively to me, uh-oh, I am the cause. I did not take that lesson very well. But, when I finally took personal responsibility for my actions, this simple lesson changed everything. This meant I was in more control of the outcome than I thought. I had to stop being the victim of what was happening. Ouch. This lesson hurt.

I changed my thinking. "If I don't like how prospects react to me, change what I say and do."

The pros know this.

Instead of looking for the perfect prospect, ready to buy, we have the power to create prospects on demand by saying and doing better things.

We are not victims. We have the power to write our future.

The next personal development lesson?

Action makes things happen.

A simple law of physics? Action makes things happen. Until we take action, nothing happens. Seems wishing, hoping, and planning don't move things forward.

Just because I set goals, it did not mean they would automatically happen. Planning alone is not enough. I would get excited about hundreds of possibilities, but thinking about things won't get the job done. On the plus side, at least I was thinking about how I could have a personally-designed future.

My biggest breakthrough?

Listening.

I spent my early career talking to people with my agenda. When they talked, I wasn't listening. I was waiting for them to finish so I can get back to telling them my message. Did others notice my agenda? Yes. They could feel it. It was all about me. My lack of interest in what they were saying was obvious. Of course, they didn't like that.

My lack of social skills had never entered my mind. All these lessons were a huge surprise for me.

What did I notice most about listening? When I listened to people with interest, they liked that. Now, creating relationships became easy. This simple change is one of the strongest ways of building rapport with others. No teacher ever brought this up in my engineering classes.

The bigger benefit happened later. Instead of me lip-syncing a pre-programmed agenda, I could now adjust what I said based on their interests. It seems people are most interested in themselves, not me or what I had to offer. Quite a surprise. This explained why no one was reacting to my wonderful sales pitch.

I couldn't talk to my prospects about what interested them, because I didn't know what interested them. I was too busy talking about me and my business.

There was some good news though. Being an introvert, it wasn't hard for me to learn to listen. I was less nervous. And then some magic happened. Prospects opened up more and told me about their problems. They wanted to fix their problems. Now there was a reason for them to listen to what I had to say.

Did I have any natural personal development skills when I started?

No. I am sure my sponsor put an ice pack on his forehead every day to dull the pain from slapping his forehead.

But what if we already have basic social skills? Wow. What a great head start on our careers. This means we could concentrate our personal development to more than the simple basics. Few people start as ill-equipped as me. But no matter where we start, we can learn and grow from there.

Here's the good news. Personal development makes us better people. Others are happy when we improve. No one is telling us, "Stop becoming a better person." It is nice to have the support of our friends and family.

Personal development is not expensive in money, but it does take time.

If we are time-poor, how can we fit personal development into our days? Jobs, family, commuting, eating, and sleeping all take time. Then what will be our plan?

Baby steps.

If reading is uncomfortable, let's start by reading one page a day. It is hard to stop after only one page, so we will naturally continue a bit longer.

Can't stand reading? How about an audiobook? Have someone read the book to us.

Prefer in-person learning experiences? Replace our golf or Internet scrolling time with a live workshop.

Every decision we make has a cost. Choosing to do one activity means not doing another activity. The cost of personal development is time.

The benefits?

We will be happier, healthier, more successful, and grow as a person. This means we can make a bigger difference in the world.

As we grow and change, our interests will upgrade to better skills. What we once found fascinating may no longer hold our attention. Our journey gets better.

Personal development is not a one-time event. It is a continuous journey that unlocks our hidden potential.

Want to make personal development almost automatic?

Choose our associations.

> "You are the average of the five people you
> spend the most time with."
>
> —Jim Rohn

Jake Pena has an alternate way to describe this. He says, "If you hang around four broke people, I guarantee you will be number five." It's a powerful way of remembering this principle. Some examples?

- If our four closest friends work out at the gym every day, we will be in shape.

- If our four closest friends are alcoholics, chances are we will have a drinking problem.
- If our four closest friends love to gossip, we will gossip too.
- If our social connections are emotional vampires, they will drain our motivation.
- If we surround ourselves with people who want to achieve more, personal development will feel great for us.

This is common sense. Even parents know this. They tell their children not to hang around gang members.

Maybe we can't affect all our associations. But with a little bit of effort, we can improve who we spend our time with. We don't have to ditch all our old friends. Just find a few good ones to add to our associations.

No permission is needed.

We can start our personal development immediately. The first step in personal development is admitting we are not perfect and can be better. That was hard for my ego. It took me years of bad results before I admitted I was the problem. Everyone around me could see it but me.

To start? It takes the willingness to take an honest look in the mirror and accept responsibility for our own actions and results. If we don't like the reflection in the mirror, then we need to change ourselves. And then, we are off on our adventure!

We can't start a new life if we keep re-living our past.

My next step?

Finally, because of my self-improvement progress, I could afford to buy books. I knew exactly the books I wanted. For me, I didn't need more inspiration. I didn't need more motivation. I desperately needed to know how to do stuff such as:

- How do I make a sale?
- How do I close prospects?
- How to overcome my fear of talking to people?
- What do leaders do?
- Where can I find more prospects?
- Why don't people listen to me?
- What is going on in my prospects' illogical minds?
- What can I say to inspire people to action?

So many questions, so much to learn, so little time. I was ready for some specific skills of exactly what to say, and exactly what to do, to improve my interactions with prospects.

This led me to Step #4: Learn network marketing skills.

STEP #4:
Learn network marketing skills

Extreme motivation with a total lack of skills equals … a fun viewing experience for our critics.

When I started network marketing, I was burning with enthusiasm. My critics entertained themselves watching me burn. Effort without direction is bad. Effort without skills is horrifying.

I was bad. And I took bad advice and make a huge strategic mistake. The advice?

"Be yourself."

What?!

Being myself is what got me into this mess in the first place! I needed to be somebody else. I needed a new strategy. I needed to learn some skills.

More ill-timed advice? "Create a vision. Focus on your passion. Think about your 'why' … and …"

This was great advice if I was in therapy, but it is not what I needed now. I was ready to go to work and actually do something, to actually talk to "live" human beings.

The big problem?

When I started network marketing, I did not know what to say and I did not know what to do. That is a recipe for failure.

Then I took even more bad advice

Weird Advice #1: "You can't say the wrong thing to the right person." Dumb advice.

Trust me, you can say the wrong thing to the right person and turn them into a bad prospect. I've done it a thousand times. Success in sponsoring is not in "finding the right person." Success is saying the right words to the prospects we talk to.

Weird Advice #2: "You can't say the right thing to the wrong person." Well, how do you think people change? They change because someone said the right thing. Why can't we be that person who says the right thing and improves someone's life? No one should be doomed for life. Now, thinking of the right thing to say to a difficult prospect might be hard. But we should at least try.

Weird Advice #3: "Just go out and get 100 no's." Well, if three "no" answers hurt, why would we want 97 more "no" answers? I didn't need to get more "no" answers. I had that mastered. I needed to learn what to say so I could get "yes" answers.

Weird Advice #4: "Every 'no' gets us closer to a 'yes.'" What? Not true. Every "no" answer only gets us closer to another "no" because we are saying the wrong thing.

At some point, even the slowest thinker realizes, "Saying the right words is what makes our sponsoring successful."

The good news?

All we have to do is find better words.

How it all changed for me.

I failed for my first year and 10 months. I accumulated no distributors and no retail customers. Others looked at me with pity, but admired my strong persistence. Persistence? The truth?

I wasn't persistent. I didn't know I could quit. I never had any downline that quit, and my sponsor didn't quit. I thought when you joined it was for life. Yes, I was naive.

But after one year and 10 months of total failure, my wife came to me and said, "How is your business coming along?" I had to tell her the truth. I said, "It is consistent."

She said, "Make it work, or do something else." She said this in a voice that suggested this advice wasn't a hint. Time to get serious.

I saw other people who were successful. I knew this business could work, but I knew I was missing something. As we know, I was missing skills. But I didn't know this. Here is how I found out.

I drove 12 hours from Chicago to Minneapolis in the snow overnight to attend a three-day seminar. My hope? They could show me what I didn't know. Unfortunately, the first two days were all about setting goals and having a good attitude. At this point I am frustrated, and frankly, my attitude was going downhill. But then the instructor took me aside. Here was our conversation.

Instructor: "So why can't you recruit new people into your business?"

Me: "Uh, the weather in Chicago is terrible. The snow is very deep and there is no place to park when people come to an opportunity meeting. Plus, we don't have opportunity meetings over the holidays. The economy is bad, inflation is high, prospects don't have any money, there is no one to talk to ..."

Instructor: "Do other networkers in Chicago recruit distributors and earn a bonus check?"

Me: "Yes."

Instructor: "Don't they have the same weather that you do?"

Me: "Uh ... uh ... yes."

Instructor: "Do they have the same prospects that you do?"

Me: "Uh ... uh ... yes."

Instructor: "Do you think that they might be saying something different to their prospects?"

Me: "Uh ... maybe ..."

Instructor: "What do you think they say that is different?"

Me: "Uh ... I don't know ..."

This wasn't going well for me. I realized that the problem was me. I was at the "scene of the crime" every time. And at that moment, I knew that I needed better skills.

I returned to Chicago and talked to the exact same people I talked to before. But, this time I changed my words. What happened? Some of the same people who didn't want to join originally, changed their minds and wanted to join. What changed? The words I said.

Oh, I finally understood.

They had not turned down my business opportunity. They had turned down how I described my business opportunity. Words made all the difference in my career.

- Same prospects.
- Same business opportunity.
- Different message.
- Different results.

How do we get these skills?

We could take the same path I did and drive 12 hours to attend a seminar. But there is an easier way. We can read a book on word skills. Attending specific skill trainings. And of course, be careful about the advice we get from others. We should ask ourselves, "Is this good advice for what I need at this time?"

We don't want more pain and frustration. We want results.

What happens if we don't learn new skills for our new profession?

Embarrassment. Huge effort with little results. Many months spent attempting to build our business and nothing to show for it. Crash and burn.

We have two choices.

First choice? We can blame outside influences, stupid prospects, the economy, the pricing, and start our network marketing career as professional victims. This isn't why we joined network marketing. We know that getting "loser" results won't get us to be in the top 1% of all income earners.

Hoping and wishing is a bad plan.

Second choice? We get serious and take action to learn the skills we need to make our business work. This is an obvious choice for us reading this book now.

Remember our goal to be in the top 1%? Our competition is weak. Most people won't try. It is easy to be in front of everyone if no one is even attempting to run.

Think of skills this way. If we wanted to learn a foreign language, a vision board or setting goals won't get us very far. That is where most people stop. They hope and wish and never do something about it.

If we took the time to learn one new word in our targeted foreign language every day, we would be far ahead of everyone who didn't try.

Now, think of all the network marketers who don't take the time to learn how to create instant rapport. Or never develop their own personalized ice breakers. Have no idea how prospects make their final decisions. Are afraid of closing because they don't know what to say. Or they hold back from doing anything because they are afraid of rejection and don't know how to avoid it.

If we have no skills, it will be hard to move forward.

Learning takes time. Talk is cheap.

Why don't our team members jump at the chance to learn new skills? They are not on the 1% path. They are taking the crowded path with the other 99%. They spend endless hours trying to get someone to talk to, but never learn what to say.

What are the skills we need to learn?

Here are four essential skills for success in network marketing. Are these the only skills? No. But we have to start somewhere. Let's start with these four skills as we will use them every time we talk to prospects.

1. Instant Rapport.

Learning how to create instant rapport is critical for success in network marketing. Without rapport, it will be difficult to build relationships and get prospects to listen to us. If prospects don't trust us or believe us, there is no need to go further into conversations about our business. If we can't "connect" with prospects, we doom ourselves to a lifetime of frustration.

We need to manipulate away their salesman alarm, their "too good to be true" filter, their negativity, their prejudices, their skepticism, their weird programs ... so our message can enter their brain. Then, they can decide if our clear message will serve them or not. Prospects have common sense.

No convincing needed. No closing needed. Our clear message either serves them today ... or not. The skill is to learn how to manipulate away all that mind garbage and prejudices, so they can hear our clear message.

2. Personalized Ice breakers.

And now, the message. Personalized ice breakers help us stand out from the crowd and make a good first impression. They help us start conversations about our business with prospects. Introducing our business into social conversations feels tricky when we start. We don't want to sound like greedy salesmen. If our ice breakers are weak, we won't have anyone to talk to.

In the beginning, my ice breakers were terrible. No one taught me good network marketing ice breakers in high school. How bad were my ice breakers? Some examples.

- "You have a loser job. I'm going to show you a better business opportunity."
- "Would you be interested in a business opportunity?"
- "I just found this great business opportunity. Shut up and listen while I explain it to you."

- "Hmmmm…. You better start working on weight loss now! This works!!!"
- "Do you want to hear about my product that can help stop your wrinkles?"
- "Want to look at my business opportunity, or are you too lazy to try something new?"
- "Are you a people person, or too shy to get ahead?"
- "Does your lack of friends hold you back?"
- I asked other networkers for their worst examples. Here are a couple of the more humorous examples.
- "You're a school teacher? You're broke ain't cha?" (Thanks to Warner Taylor.)
- "If you were to start brushing your teeth, would you try my toothpaste?" (Thanks to Michael Bonner.)
- Bob Patterson shared a few more.
- "Hi, take this material and read it. Can I call you tomorrow to see if you liked what you saw?"
- "Excuse me. I know you don't know me, but I have a ground floor opportunity. Give me your number and I'll call you."
- "Hi, my name is Bob. I want to show you something. Would Monday at 4 pm or Wednesday at 2 pm be better for you?"
- "I know this sounds crazy, but I'm expanding my business right here. Want to watch a quick video while we're waiting in this checkout line"?

Networkers have a great sense of humor!

There are books about ice breakers. We want to have a huge stack of ready-to-use ice breakers so that we can choose the right ice breaker for the right situation. Think of ice breakers as our introductory offer. A basic component in our toolbox.

After the rapport skill, our ice breakers will be the second most important skill in our toolbox. A bad ice breaker can doom our chances. A bad ice breaker makes it easy for our prospects to be skeptical and resist everything we say. Here is an example.

Bad ice breaker: "Have I got a great deal for you."

And now, our prospects think:

- "You're not going to trick me into buying anything."
- "I'm not stupid, you know."
- "I don't believe a word you say."
- "You're just trying to take advantage of me."
- "I don't have time for this."
- "This is a scam, isn't it?"
- "I won't fall for this."
- "This is a waste of time."
- "I don't want what you are selling."
- "Get out of my house!"

Could we say better things? Of course. That is why we should study and master ice breakers. Here are a couple to start us in the right direction.

- "Jobs interfere with the week."
- "We can change our life with a four-day week."
- "Retirement is hard, but there is a pension solution."
- "I just found out how to get an extra paycheck."

- "How to earn more money part-time than our boss does full-time."

3. Decision Making.

Understanding how humans make decisions is key to helping prospects choose our product, service, or opportunity. After all, isn't that our job? To get prospects to make a "yes" decision? If we don't know how prospects make decisions, how can we lead them through the process? Having a job, and not knowing how to do that job ... well, that would be bad.

If you asked me when I started in network marketing how prospects made decisions, I would take wild guesses such as:

- They wait for lightning to strike.
- They listen to the little voices inside their heads.
- They wait for a flash of inspiration or a sign.
- It was some sort of hormone thing.
- Today's horoscope?
- Coin flips? Tea leaves?
- 15,000 reasons for, and 14,000 reasons against. (My favorite.)
- They sit through a 30-minute presentation, watch company videos, and look at PowerPoint slides. Then they listen to testimonials and carefully weigh the pros and cons, and then ... make a final logical decision based on the facts.

Guessing at stuff isn't a skill.

This is the time we start learning how minds make decisions on emotion, not logic. So, we will want to appeal to their emotional brain first. Later, we can present facts to their logical brain so that they can justify their decisions. We must get prospects to decide they want what we have to offer emotionally as our first step.

We have a brain. So do our prospects. We might as well figure out how the brain works because that is where we do our work.

4. Closing.

Knowing how to close a sale is essential for success in network marketing. This is what we get paid to do. If we don't know how to ask for the sale, we'll miss out on opportunities, and of course, never get paid. Since fear of rejection holds many of us back, we will want to learn rejection-free, totally-safe closing techniques. If we don't know how to do this, now would be the perfect time to learn methods such as the options approach, the binary choices, and more.

As professionals, we want to have several "go-to" closing phrases that work for us. For example, I learned to pre-close better by using trained phrases such as:

- "Before I show you how this works, let me tell you what happened to me."
- "Most people I show this business to, get excited about it and want to join."
- "When we are tired of commuting, this is what we look for."

There are many other skills we can learn that will help us build our business. These four core skills are a good place to start.

What are other skills professional network marketers want to learn to be in the top 1%?

5. The four color personalities.

One of the most popular skills. Why? Because not only is this fun to do, but we will use the skill for every human encounter for the rest of our lives. This is a simple skill to learn. We can customize what we say to how our prospects think. Not every prospect thinks and sees the world in the same way. For example, some prospects feel motivated to share our opportunity because it helps others. Others feel excited about our opportunity because it is so much fun. When we re-word our offers to align with how they view the world, magic happens. Yes, there are at least four different ways to rephrase what we say.

6. How to meet new people.

When I started, no one told me I should smile. I thought I should be serious. Whoops! But it got worse. I avoided eye contact. Did I know about open-ended questions? No. Why I should ask questions? No. Be interested in what they are saying? No. I wanted to tell prospects about my business. Why waste time as I wanted to get to my important presentation.

And what were these social skills everyone was talking about? If it wasn't for someone encouraging me to read the book, "How to Win Friends and Influence People" ... I would have never known how to even start.

7. How to be a good listener.

The purpose of our business is to solve our prospects' problems. How can we know their problems if we don't listen? Rude salespeople have a "one size fits all" sales presentation. The news gets even better. Prospects love people who listen to them. The basics are simple. Pay attention, don't interrupt, be patient, and reflect back what we hear. Listen for the message instead of thinking of what we want to say next. That is so hard to do. Once we master these simple listening basics, we can grow into higher-level active listening skills that rock. This is where the real magic happens.

8. Asking Questions.

The next skill is how to ask questions. This may seem like a no-brainer, but we never get training on how to properly ask questions. We will want to learn how to ask open-ended questions, leading questions, and probing questions. These types of questions will help us to discover our prospects' problems and how we can best serve them. Prospects love answering questions because they get to talk about themselves.

9. Magic sequences of words.

Some phrases create mistrust and skepticism. Other phrases build trust and open minds.

I didn't know the power of changing a few words. How did I discover this? I saw my "not interested" prospects join other network marketers who used different words. Huh? Time for me to learn better words. Here is an example.

I used to say, "Would you be interested in …?" Prospects told me they were not interested.

I learned to re-word that question to, "Would it be okay if …?" What happened? Prospects normally agreed. Instant magic. I could not believe the difference.

Here are some examples of the magic sequences of words Keith and I use a lot.

- Most people. (Most people want to be their own boss.)
- Everybody knows. (Everybody knows it is hard to get by on one paycheck.)
- Everybody says. (Everybody says it's almost impossible to get rich on a salaried job.)
- There is an old saying. (There is an old saying. Two paychecks are better than one.)
- There are two types of people in the world. (There are two types of people in the world. Those that spent two hours commuting to work every day, and those that can spend those two hours with their children.)
- Are you okay with …? (Are you okay with having to work until age 67 before you can retire?)

This list could be endless. We have heard phrases like these many times before, but didn't realize they were magical.

- I have some good news and some bad news.
- Before I show you how this works, let me tell you what happened to me.
- So what is going to be easier for you?

Keith and I have written books about first sentences and getting prospects' attention using these phrases. These phrases get attention, action, and results.

10. Motivation.

Not motivated? Then now is the time to learn that skill. Instead of wishing for mythical spirits of inspiration or waiting for an outside stimulus, we can learn how to motivate ourselves on demand. Some crazy, fun networkers might consider:

- 440-volt coffee?
- Espresso inhalers?
- Intravenous energy drinks?
- 100-decibel heavy metal music?
- Eat a live frog for breakfast?
- Insult our mother-in-law?

Of course, these short-term techniques come with a risk.

Maybe we are more "sensible" about managing our motivation. We could use meditation, affirmations, change our point of view, exercise, and more.

These ideas are a start. We could take a different direction and learn how to make our business-building activities fun. Then there would be no need for motivation. We would look forward to our activities.

What is the default solution for the 99%?

Complain. Ask for someone to change the rules. Whine in the hopes of getting rich. Yeah, we don't want to go down that path. We want to move forward to be in the top 1%.

11. Needs vs. wants.

Bad news. Our team members want to go to people who "need" our products, services, or opportunity. Unfortunately, many of these people don't "want" what we offer. This dooms our team to constant follow-up, convincing, and high-pressure selling to reluctant prospects. This is discouraging. We want to use proper stories and lessons to help them focus on prospects who "want" what we offer. Does this take time? Yes, but it is so worth it.

Marketing what we offer to people who want what we offer is good business sense. We only have 24 hours a day. After a job, family, and sleep, there isn't much time left. We want to spend those few remaining hours talking to people who want what we have to offer.

12. Soundbites.

Attention spans are short. Sometimes less than a sentence. Sad but true. But soundbites can become a superpower. We say a few words or a short phrase. Not only will our phrase create images in our prospects' minds, but also trigger a strong emotional response that leads to an instant decision. Magic. We can pass on these tested soundbites to our team to use. No training needed. Just say the soundbite and let the soundbite do its magic. Some quick examples of soundbites?

- Turn your body into a fat-burning machine.
- Dream-sucking vampire boss.
- One facial wrinkle away from looking like a prune.
- If you don't take care of your body, then where are you going to live?

- Stop putting chemicals inside your children's mouths when they brush their teeth.

- Take 5-star holidays for the price of a budget hotel.

- Never curse tangled hair again.

- The 3-minute makeup trick that makes mornings easy.

- Our chocolate shakes are like having dessert for breakfast.

- Travel like a millionaire on a thrift store budget.

- Lose weight while eating chocolate.

- Is our face our best first impression?

- Stop sending generic greeting cards that show we don't care.

- Fall asleep within seven minutes of our heads touching the pillow.

We will want plenty of personalized soundbites for a business.

13. Stories.

We can be lifelong students of story skills. Stories communicate at a much higher level in the human brain. Stories are the preferred method of understanding for our prospects, so why wouldn't we use them?

If we are going to use stories, maybe we should learn a little bit about story structure, the power of word pictures, how to make our stories shorter and more engaging, and take our story skills to a whole new level. A few basic lessons can improve our story communication skills with huge gains.

Movies are more engaging than lectures. What do children want to hear before bedtime? Stories. They beg for stories. Stories are one of the fastest ways to learn.

One good story can create a lifetime of results.

14. Prospecting.

Where to go. What to look for. What to say. How to get referrals. The best strategies. Creating appointments. Follow up, and more.

If we can't prospect, we won't have anyone to talk to.

An essential skill for the top 1%.

15. Objections.

This is huge. Deep breath. Let's talk about those energy-killing words our prospects might choose. We will never be in the 1% if we live in fear of objections. Prospects will notice our nervous twitching.

We can't take objections personally. If we get defensive, we send the wrong signal to our prospects. Instead, let's accept the fact that everyone has objections from time to time. Here is a classic example.

Friend: "Want to go jogging with me?"

Big Al: "No." (This is an objection. I am allergic to jogging. My face turns red, I get a rapid heartbeat, and I break out into a sweat.)

Friend: "Then how about walking with me to get some donuts?"

Big Al: "I will hold the door open for you so you can catch up with me."

Yes. We are still friends. Objections are not a personal rejection. We don't reject our friends, but we may reject what they offer.

Always consider our offers as gifting an additional option for our prospects' lives. This protects us from feeling bad when our prospects don't want our offer now. It happens.

But here is the good news about using the word, "Options." It changes our prospects' attitude towards what we offer. Feel the difference between these two scenarios.

Us: "I want to give you a presentation."

Prospects: "Gasp!" Blood leaves their faces. They grasp at their heart spasms. They know a sales pitch is coming, and that means we will try to close them at the end. Our prospects immediately begin looking for reasons why our presentation won't work. They want ammunition to defend themselves from evil, high-pressure salesmen. Yes, we cause our prospects to look for reasons why our offer won't work.

Us: "I want to give you another option."

Prospects: "Option?" <Smile.> That means no pressure. They are in control. They can choose to take this option or not. No bad feelings. But wait! The only way this option can have value for them is if they take the option. Now they look for ways our option can work. We cause our prospects to want what we will offer.

But what if we get the same objections over and over?

That is a sign. Heed the warning. This is more than a hint.

We could be the cause. While we may say the wrong words, the most common reason is a lack of rapport. Our prospects feel disconnected from us. They feel we think differently. Our lack of understanding of our most basic skills has now come back to haunt us.

16. The principle of reaction.

Have we ever experienced these events?

1. We walk into a store, and the sales clerk asks us, "Can I help you?" What is our automatic answer? "Oh no, I am just looking."

2. We pass someone while walking, and the person casually says, "Hi." What is our automatic response? "Hi." No thinking involved.

3. We smile as we enter the elevator. Their automatic response? They smile back.

4. When we are talking with someone, and they say something that we agree with, what is our natural response? "Me too!" We don't even think about it.

5. When someone asks, "How are you?" Most people reply, "I am fine, and you?"

Do we see a pattern?

These responses are examples of automatic programs in our human brains. These control our behaviors automatically, without thinking about them. And they are powerful.

Humans go through life reacting, reacting, and reacting.

Now, here is the question.

We meet a prospect. Does our prospect's behavior have anything to do with the prospect? Or does our prospect's behavior have everything to do with what we say and what we do?

Oh.

Our prospects react to us.

At the very least we should be thinking, "If I don't like how prospects react to me, change what I say and do."

Instead of looking for the perfect prospect, ready to buy, we have the power to create prospects on demand by saying and doing better things.

We are not victims. We have the power to write our future. Our prospects' behavior is a reaction to us.

And we haven't even got to basic leadership skills yet!

Oh my. So much to learn, so little time. We will want to learn as fast and as efficiently as possible.

Can we learn these skills by "trial and error?" Yes. We learn and remember from personal experience. But ... "trial and error" is painful. Rejection and failure hurt. And it gets worse. "Trial and error" takes too long. No one wants to delay launcher bonus checks for months or years.

Confucius said this:

By three methods we may learn wisdom.

First, by reflection, which is noblest.

Second, by imitation, which is easiest.

Third, by experience, which is the bitterest.

Choice #2 looks pretty good. We will want to learn the skills for our network marketing careers fast.

To be in the top 1%, we want to learn the right words to say, and the right actions to take to be successful. Skills make the difference in our careers. It is the secret ingredient many networkers miss.

STEP #5: Hands-on experience.

You and I will compete in a jujitsu match in 30 days. We are both beginners and have no skills or knowledge of jujitsu.

Here is my master plan. I will read books, take notes, watch Jackie Chan movies, create a vision board, and psych myself up for the big match. Oh, and I will have a secret affirmation that I will chant every morning.

Your plan? Take a jujitsu lesson every day. Learn one new move every day. Practice with your instructor, and try it with some fellow students.

Now, what do you think will happen in our jujitsu match in 30 days? I can see the future already, so I am going to buy extra life insurance. This is going to be ugly.

Learning is different than doing.

Knowing all the right answers is useless if we are not in action.

We are like rabid fans at a football game, sitting in the stands, yelling at the players who are taking action. Do we have good advice? It doesn't matter. If we are not in the game, it is all talk.

Learn, practice, do.

In step #4, we learned skills of exactly what to say and exactly what to do. That is not enough. We should practice everything that we learn, get experience, and then we will build confidence to do this effectively in real life.

Can we remember how we learned to swim? Did we read a book, watch a movie, and then jump into the deep end of the pool? If that was our plan, we know exactly how we felt standing on the edge of the pool before our first jump. We felt terrified. No experience. No confidence. Total fear. Thank goodness this was not our stupid plan.

How did we learn to swim? Our first lesson was how to hold our breath under the water. Later, how to open our eyes under the water. Next, we learned to move our arms and legs to propel ourselves and keep us afloat. Again, we practiced near the edge of the pool. Letting go of the edge of the pool was scary. With experience, soon we could dog paddle and keep ourselves afloat.

Baby steps.

Can we remember how we learned to ride a bicycle? Did we read a book, watch a few motorcycle races from the stands, and dream of being a great two-wheel legend? No. What did we do?

We learned to sit on our bicycle seat with both feet planted firmly on the ground. In time, we started to feel a bit off balance. Soon we could coast on our bicycles for a few seconds. If we had training wheels, they came off after we had more experience and confidence.

Can we remember how we learned to use the Internet? No, we didn't read a book. We learned one little thing, tried it, practiced it, and over time we learn to navigate the Internet and find the information we want.

Learning is the same as "not learning" ... if we cannot put our skills to use.

We have to put our new knowledge to work. That is obvious, but why don't we?

Fear.

This is why we have to take baby steps.

My friend, Jerry Clark, tells this story from early in his career. He was the company trainer. Every Saturday he taught a beginners' class on personalities. Every Saturday, the exact same class. When new distributors joined during the week, they attended the Saturday morning class to learn and start their business.

But Jerry noticed something strange. In addition to the new distributors attending every Saturday, there were a few older distributors that came every Saturday, week after week. The class content was always the same. So why did these older distributors come back week after week?

Jerry discovered their fear. They found it easier to pretend they needed to review the information again than to go out and actually talk to a "live" prospect.

I can relate to that feeling. Can you?

This is why some networkers default to watching cat videos on the Internet instead of making phone calls to get an appointment. This is why some networkers become professional students, and never talk to anyone.

When we recognize and accept this reality, we can put a plan in motion to fix this problem. The plan?

Baby steps.

What are the three steps?

1. Learn.
2. Practice.
3. Do.

Okay, learning is the easy part. No rejection or fear. Plenty of books, audios, and courses with all the tips and skill strategies we need. This book we are reading right now is part of our "Learn" phase. We want to know what works so we can take effective action. Results are what count.

Step #2 is practice. This step is where we gain confidence to overcome our fear. This is where we can test what works and what doesn't work for us. The most effective way to increase our chances of success is to decrease our risk of failure. How do we do that?

Baby steps.

Remember how we learned to swim? We practiced at the edge of the pool. We got used to the feeling of being in the water.

Remember how we learned to ride a bicycle? We spent time sitting on the bicycle seat, coasting for a few seconds, and with time, built confidence. Only then did we take our bicycle out in the street for our first big ride.

Now, how can we practice network marketing?

We can practice under controlled conditions with our sponsor or fellow distributors. That is safe. But, we can stretch ourselves and our comfort zones a bit more. We can practice with our family or close associates. Here is an example.

We want to learn how to use an options close so our prospects can make an immediate decision. They will feel good because they will have complete control over their choice. And because we gave them choices, it appears we are not attached to the outcome.

Now there is less chance that we will feel embarrassed if they say "no" to our offer. How would this sound if we were talking to a prospect?

Us: "So what is going to be easier for you? To start a part-time business with us this evening, or to continue trying to get by on one paycheck?"

A nice option. Our prospect can choose. We don't feel vulnerable or embarrassed if the prospect chooses not to join us this evening. We don't feel stress or panic. We know our offer is better than getting by on one paycheck. Most prospects will agree. And if one prospect doesn't agree, it might still be good as this prospect could be having other, more serious problems.

But, where can we practice this?

With our children! I love practicing with my grandchildren. So much fun. Here's what I could say to my granddaughter at dinner this evening.

"So what is going to be easier for you? To eat your vegetables now, or never have a Wi-Fi password again?"

Okay. A little cruel, but we will remember this example. Every technique we practice gives us more confidence. We can practice word phrases, smiles, body language, and all of the communication skills safely with family and friends.

The more we practice, the more experience we get. Fear melts away when we have experience.

Prospecting with strangers.

Baby steps.

Step #3 is to do.

Before the Internet and expensive long-distance phone calls, most prospecting was done in person. This is scary for introverts. This is terrifying for us who are socially challenged.

Going door-to-door, prospecting in office buildings and shopping malls, making cold calls to total strangers ... ugh! Dental surgery sounded more inviting to me. I didn't know anyone. I had just moved to a new city.

My first few tries looked like a nervous 15-year-old boy asking for his first date. I will spare you the ugly details of my crushing defeats.

What could I do to get experience in a safer environment?

Networking events to the rescue.

The good news? Everyone at networking events wants to be there. They want to have a conversation. This was a baby step for me. Now I would be surrounded by people I could talk to, but of course, I was still scared.

When we try new things we get experience. I learned that if I didn't know what to say, it didn't matter. People at these networking events want to do all the talking. They enjoy talking at me and shoving business cards into my face. I could stand and smile while trying to think of something intelligent to say, if they ever allowed me to talk.

Baby steps.

In time, I got better. I learned that if I asked a question, people would talk even more. The more others talked, the more they liked me. A few people eventually asked me what I did. Huge progress and this small step built my confidence.

At first, I was trying to get comfortable in face-to-face conversation. I wasn't trying to sell anything. After a lot of practice, I learned how to introduce my business into the conversation without a lot of panic.

What happens when we get more experience from step #3? From doing?

We experience different types of reactions when we use the new skill that we learned. For example, with the options close that we use with prospects, there are only a few predictable responses. Now when we hear these predictable responses, we don't panic. We are not surprised.

Will our confidence rub off on our prospects? Yes. They will feel more confident in us. We will get less negativity and better results.

Doing, taking action, gives us experience.

Baby steps rock!

Meeting new people at networking events became my go-to way of finding prospects and building new relationships. Through practice, low-risk encounters, and experience, I learned the best way for me as a shy introvert was to approach people at networking events. Then, I developed a plan.

#1. Find the shyest people at the event. They have their backs to the wall, standing uncomfortably alone, and pretend to look at their cell phones as if someone cared enough to message them. I know they would feel better if they were talking to me instead of feeling so self-conscious.

#2. I could ask them their name, but that might scare them. Instead, I start with my name first so that they will feel more comfortable. I say, "Hi. My name is Big Al. What is your name?"

#3. And now? Time to establish some rapport. Chat about things we have in common. We could say, "This networking event location was very hard to find." Or, we could say, "I don't know anyone here. Everyone is a stranger."

The good news?

This shy stranger wants to continue the conversation. This is much better than standing alone. My little secret? Make sure I find a shy person who is even more scared than me.

If I didn't try to sell, if I didn't try to close, I could have a conversation with no rejection. I needed experience talking to people so that I wouldn't be so nervous in the future. Yes, I had a long way to go in my career, but starting is the first step.

Many people have this step mastered, the ability to have a conversation without sweating. But if we don't? Time to take action and learn how to do it.

With experience comes confidence. We know most people will react to us in a few predictable ways. We learn these ways by observing with our trial and error experience. Now, we won't be surprised by an unusual question or reaction. It is the fear of the unknown that can paralyze us from taking action. We like feeling comfortable.

So how do we get out of our comfort zone to gain this important experience?

Let's admit it. We worry about what other people think about us. This is normal. Humans are social. We want to be accepted by our group of peers. No one wants to be an outcast. Even brave, ultra-confident superstars secretly worry about what others think of them. So how do we manage this feeling?

This is hard. So instead of trying to fool or trick our feelings, let's get our experience in safe environments. We want situations where we will have less fear of rejection and don't have to worry what other people think. An example?

Let's imagine we are afraid of closing. We don't ask closing questions because we don't want to feel bad if our prospects say, "No." We know this hurts our career, so how will we get more experience with closing questions to build our confidence?

Imagine we are a waiter at a restaurant. We could say, "Would you like to order dessert tonight?" We can learn to manage our feelings by imagining this closing request is an option. The restaurant customers can make a choice to add 1,000 calories to their waistline this evening, or not. Their decision is about their waistline, not if we are being personally rejected. Feel better?

If this doesn't work, let's try a different mindset. Again, let's ask the same question, "Would you like to order dessert tonight?" This time we are asking the question because we are curious. Their answer satisfies our curiosity and doesn't feel like a personal rejection.

We could even make a game of this. We could test our mind-reading skills. Before we ask this closing question, we try to guess what they will say. Now we took our focus away from our personal feelings and placed our focus on testing our mind-reading skills. This might be the little step we need to move forward and get the experience we need.

Oh, but we say to ourselves, "I am not a waiter. What else could I do?"

Let's volunteer. Why volunteer? Yes, volunteering will make the world a better place, but that is not our reason. People are nice to volunteers. If people are rude to volunteers, the volunteers quit. So, we should expect nice interactions.

Adult education classes work well. Instant rapport with our fellow students. We all want to learn. And think about the people that attend adult education classes. They take action. They want more in their lives. This is a great place to connect with quality prospects for our business.

And if we are planning, maybe we should take an adult education class on salesmanship instead of basket weaving. That is what I did. The good news? None of my fellow classmates ever said this, "I don't want to be a salesman."

But all of these examples are in-person. Today, we live in an online world. Think of the possibilities. We can test our people skills with a simple chat message. Later, when we are braver, we can talk. Over time, we could even do a video call.

Baby steps.

Start small. Get some experience within our comfort zone.

We don't have to tell lies to our brains, "I am brave. I am courageous. I am thick-skinned. I don't care what others think."

Instead, just like working out in a gym, we can slowly build our muscles and succeed. We don't have to be gifted with courage and confidence. We can learn and grow with baby steps.

Take action. We learned skills in Step #4. We know what works. Nothing is going to happen until we take action.

If we are feeling fear right now, just remember.

Baby steps.

STEP #6:
Teach our professional networking skills to others.

Q. What is the best way to master our network marketing skills?

A. To teach these skills.

Remember the incompetent physics class substitute teacher from high school? The one who studied ancient Greek literature in college?

"Here is how the theory of relativity works. There is some energy, some mass, and we mix it with a dash of the speed of light and then ... some magic happens."

We didn't learn anything that day. Our substitute teacher was clueless.

Now, if a substitute teacher didn't know how to teach physics, there is a good chance we learned nothing. We can't teach what we don't know.

The network marketing motivational speakers scream, "Duplicate! It is all about duplication!"

But if we duplicate garbage, pass on skills that don't work, we won't get to the top 1% of network marketing.

When we prepare ourselves to teach, we will improve.

Here are seven reasons why teaching our network marketing skills will make us better.

Reason #1. When we have to explain a skill, we must understand it.

Teaching forces us to be clear. No one has the time to listen to us ramble and not get to the point. Our listeners can identify vague incompetencies, fluff, and filler words. If we don't know or understand what we are doing, teaching exposes our weaknesses. Our students' reactions? A cringing face, or a blank stare into space. Some will start playing games on their cell phones.

These reactions are clues that we are faking it. People react to half-hearted explanations and feel that we don't care, that we didn't respect them enough to prepare a decent explanation.

We have to study and prepare for our lessons? Yes. We can't fake skill.

Reason #2. Teaching helps us break down a skill into easier-to-understand parts.

Skills seem complicated to new people. When we explain a skill, we need to break it down into smaller pieces. For example, imagine we want to teach the skill of creating rapport with prospects.

Where would we start? Why do we have multiple steps? Could we give options of different ways? Do we start with a general explanation and then break down each component? Let's try this for an example outline of how we will teach the skill of rapport.

1. Why rapport is important.

2. What happens when we don't have rapport.

3. Our goal is for prospects to trust us and believe the good things we say.

4. We want our prospects to feel that we understand them.

5. We want our prospects to feel that we view the world from the same perspective.

6. We must remove our prospects' prejudices and biases.

7. What is the best way to signal we have a similar viewpoint.

8. Pick a common fact to signal agreement.

9. Smile.

10. Learn magic word phrases that connect with their minds.

When we break the skill down into tiny steps, this means we understand it. We won't sound like that clueless substitute physics teacher.

A good exercise is to try to teach this skill to a 7-year-old. A great challenge.

Reason #3. Teaching forces us to organize our thoughts into a logical order.

There is nothing more frustrating for our listeners than a stream of consciousness, crazy, random explanation that leads to nowhere. Listeners won't have patience with us when they realize we didn't prepare.

In the previous example for the rapport skill, the ten-step outline kept us on track. We helped our listeners learn in bite-sized steps. A well-organized presentation makes us sound credible so others will take our teaching seriously. We want our listeners to believe what we say, and then put it into action.

Breaking a skill down into bite-sized pieces forces us to have a deeper understanding of every step of the process. This gives us confidence when we use the skill ourselves.

What happens when we are not organized and fake our understanding of a skill? We make up random advice on the rapport skill such as:

- Just be yourself.
- Have personality.
- It is all about your intention.
- Be sincere.

That sounds good, but isn't helpful for someone new. Vague and disorganized advice is a waste of time.

Reason #4. Teaching helps us understand and learn more about our skill.

Teaching points out the information gaps we have. Try explaining something we don't know to listeners. It gets obvious fast that we are missing important steps. We know the feeling. We are explaining and then, "Uh-oh." And uncomfortable long pause. That is the moment we know we are at loss for what to say next. This embarrassment motivates us to learn the missing gaps in our information about this skill.

Good teachers master their material backwards and forwards. If we can't explain the basics of a basic skill, how will we get others to do it?

For example, we are teaching the skill about rapport. We say, "Here are the reasons our prospects don't trust us or believe us."

Brain freeze. Panic. Embarrassment. Whoops. Information gap. We don't know what to say next.

To prevent future embarrassment, we research deeper into our skill and learn everything we can. Our expertise not only makes us feel confident, but also gives our listeners confidence in us. They want to follow the advice of leaders who knows what they are talking about.

The more we teach the skill, the more information gaps we will notice. We need to be able to answer every objection and counter every argument.

Reason #5. Teaching helps us learn from our listeners' feedback.

Do our listeners take notes and politely fade away? Hmmm, this means we are not effective. A bad sign.

Do our listeners feel confused and ask a lot of questions? This shows us where we are unclear and we need to focus more.

Do our listeners ask us questions that we never thought about? Oh, this is good. We might only have understood the skill from our viewpoint. We have a different background and skillset than our listeners. This again helps us expand our knowledge and mastery of this skill. Getting this immediate feedback is invaluable.

Even criticism helps us. Challenging what we know helps us understand deeper. How do we feel when our listeners disagree with one of our key points? Do we defend our position, or do we consider this a learning opportunity? We should ask ourselves, "What did I say to trigger this reaction?"

Teaching can be a giant mastermind where we learn from many viewpoints and backgrounds. Our best learning moments can come from being challenged. This causes us to rethink and re-evaluate what we thought was true.

Reason #6. Teaching solidifies our skill through the power of repetition.

Repetition is a great way to learn. But, we want to make sure that we are repeating the right things. That is why in Step #4, we learned the skills that actually work. To continue perfecting the wrong mistake is not making progress.

For example, what if this was my closing statement? "Any idiot can see this is a great opportunity. Do you have a problem with that?"

This closing statement would be a mistake. If I practice and repeat this closing statement over and over, this means I memorized the wrong thing. We want to make sure that we practice the power of repetition on skills that work.

Here is why we should love repetition. We don't have to think what comes next. Instead, we can put our mind's focus on how our prospect reacts. We can be a focused listener when our prospect talks, instead of worrying what are the next words in our presentation.

This is why the pros appear calmer and more confident when talking to prospects. They have muscle memory. So many of their high-level skills are automatic. They don't have to waste precious brain resources on remembering what comes next.

Repetition can help solidify a mental checklist so that we don't leave something out.

Bottom line? The repetition of the skills through teaching takes us to a higher level.

Reason #7. Teaching will help build our team members into leaders.

When our team members start with us, how many solid network marketing skills will they have? Few, if any.

Where will they learn the skills? From us.

Our job is to turn ordinary team members into leaders. That is the fastest way to get to the top 1%. The good news is that we don't have to do this alone. Our team will be a reflection of our growing professionalism and skills. The faster we grow, the faster they will grow too.

Want to get the ultimate leverage? We will want to teach teachers, who teach other teachers, who teach other teachers, to multiply our effect in our business.

The math is simple. We grow faster with the help of others.

STEP #7:
Make our successful activities a habit.

Making decisions is hard. Making decisions when we feel tired or discouraged is even harder. Some people complain about decision fatigue and how it makes their willpower weaker.

How do we make better decisions? Willpower. Motivation. Vision. Persistence and more. But, if we have to do these things every day, our chances of failure increase.

But, there is another way. We can create habits.

Habits happen automatically, no thinking is involved. We don't have to choose if we want to do this today or not. Our subconscious mind just accepts this is how things are, and gets on with whatever activity we must do. Some habit examples?

How many of us have a habit of putting clothes on in the morning before we leave our homes? When was the last time we forgot? Do we have to motivate ourselves to put on our clothes? Do we need a vision board to keep us focused? No. A checklist? No. Putting on clothes in the morning is a habit.

Do we have a habit of brushing our teeth? Is this an automatic part of our morning and evening routine? We don't have to argue with ourselves to brush our teeth. It is a habit.

But, what about going to work on Monday mornings? Is that a habit? Yes. But here is what is different. We don't enjoy that habit. We want to sleep longer or continue celebrating our weekend.

There is an important lesson here. It is easier to keep our habits if we enjoy our habits.

Natural is better than forced.

We want our success to feel effortless and natural. Our daily activities should be things we enjoy doing. No one needs extra motivation to do what we enjoy.

Children don't have to force themselves to wake up on Saturday morning to enjoy the weekends. They don't have "to-do" lists. They don't micromanage their days into 15-minute chunks of organized key performance statistics.

Look at this Venn diagram from our book, "The Happy Network Marketer."

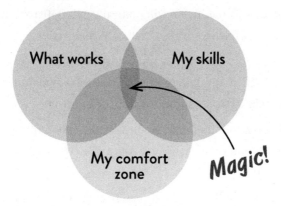

The first circle represents skills that work. The second circle represents skills that are within our level of competency. Yes, there are many skills that work that we can't personally do. Maybe our background or personal knowledge isn't good enough.

Ah, but the third circle is the important circle.

The third circle represents the skills that make us feel happy daily.

What about skills or activities that make us unhappy? This is why many people hate their jobs. They have to rely on constant motivation. Instead, let's pick the activities that bring us joy.

Do we see where these three circles overlap? Yes, this is where the magic happens.

These are the activities that we want to make into our daily habits. We will do these activities automatically, without having to make conscious decisions every time we do them.

Here is a quick example. To build our business, we need to prospect regularly. If our method of prospecting feels outside of our comfort zone, we will fatigue quickly. If our method of prospecting makes us happy, we will naturally gravitate to that activity daily. We won't have to drag ourselves to take action.

Some people love social media. They are on every possible platform. Their natural method of prospecting is to add value first and build relationships second with their connections.

If we force them into an uncomfortable cold-calling script, no matter how good their results are, they will eventually give up. No one likes continuous pain.

Other people love making new friends at networking events and coffee shops where they live. They would rather talk to someone one-on-one than to hide behind a computer screen. If we force them into a social media pitchfest, they will hate their daily prospecting activity and get discouraged.

Ask ourselves, "Of all the possible activities we could do to build our business, which activities bring us joy?" Those activities can become natural habits that move us forward to our success.

I am a better "giver" than a "closer."

When I started network marketing, my viewpoint was, "Convince people to buy or join." Every encounter with a prospect was a "win/lose", or "live or die" situation. I hated this. Not only did I not enjoy it, but I lost most of the time. This definitely would not be sustainable over a long career.

But what did I enjoy? What made me feel great?

Giving.

My new viewpoint when presenting to prospects? "I will gift my prospects with one more option for their lives."

This means my prospects can keep their lives the same, and continue struggling with their problems. Or, they can choose the wonderful option I gifted to them.

Every day became fun. I spent my time looking for new people to gift my option of a great part-time business. I couldn't think of anything more fun to do.

What happened? I gave my option to more people, and more people joined me than when I was in "convince mode." Now, every day was fun. No depressing activities that would deplete my energy. I couldn't wait to share more.

Examples of closing that worked best for me? Here are two of my favorite option closes.

- "So what is going to be easier for you? Starting your part-time business now, or continue trying to get by on one paycheck?"

- "Does it make sense to have a part-time business that can grow, instead of working a part-time job for the rest of our lives?"

These phrases made me feel great. I was gifting one more option for my prospects' lives. No rejection or bad feelings for me. I allowed my prospects to choose the great option I presented, or if they preferred, they could keep their problems and continue their lives the same.

It's not about making constant decisions. It's about creating habits! Habits of activities we love to do. I created a habit of gifting options.

When we have habits, we will have the energy and desire to continue taking massive action. We become unstoppable! We have smiles on our faces.

We can't control events.

Events happen. Good events, and bad events too. Frustration is wishing we could go back in time to change the past. Our current skill sets don't include time travel. We can't redesign the past. We all know people who insist on re-living their past painful events over and over again, never letting go. They refuse to let go of those bad feelings, and refuse to move forward in their lives.

And what about the future? Worrying is projecting negative events that might happen, and now we feel our energy slowly sucked away. This doesn't sound like much fun either. This is an ugly career path.

Controlling outside events is difficult. No one has complete control of everything. Instead, let's focus our thoughts and efforts on what is within our control, our reactions to outside events.

While it's unpleasant to experience negative events, knowing that we're taking steps to make a difference going forward can help us feel better.

This is a great habit to create. Maybe we could make a mantra that we could say to ourselves such as, "This happened. What can I do moving forward?"

Then, feel glad that we have the ability to choose our reactions.

Turn good advice into habits.

Simon Chen wrote a book, "The Consistency Pill." Jim Packard and George Campbell wrote a book, "The Consistency Chain for Network Marketing." There is strength when we harness the power of habits. Consistency rocks. Think of consistency this way. If we are pointed in the right direction, and are doing the right things with our skills, every little effort we do accumulates and moves us closer to our destination. It is hard to go wrong when we are moving in the right direction. Our once-every-so-often prospecting won't produce enough results to build us to the top 1%.

The question is, "How can I do a consistent activity long enough so that it will eventually become a habit?"

The answer? Make sure we choose an activity that we love to do. Why stop doing what we enjoy?

Could we build our business by doing cold calls to strangers? Yes. Would we look forward to this and feel it is fun? For most of us, no. Chances are this will never become a habit that we feel compelled to do every morning because it makes us happy.

What other way could we make contact with prospects that would be more fun? If we could find that activity, something we enjoy, our consistency is almost guaranteed. We can see a great habit on the horizon.

Maybe our way is this. We love coffee. The best part of our day at work? Coffee breaks. We can chat with our coworkers while enjoying caffeine.

We could redefine our business as meeting prospects over coffee six times a day. We get to visit new coffee shops, try new coffee flavors, and have the time of our life meeting new and interesting people over coffee. We can't wait to meet someone new over coffee every day. We love this habit. And the power of consistency rides along with our new habit.

The easiest way to build a new habit is to make sure we love the activity. That makes consistency automatic.

If we need a little extra push, then we could do this. Find a friend or family member who wants to form the same habit. It's easier to create a new habit with an accountability partner who wants the same habit also. What a great way to pull a team member up to our level.

Love the process ... not the goal.

"Desire is a contract that you make with yourself
to be unhappy until you get what you want."

—Naval Ravikant

Ouch!!!

Don't set a one-year goal and tell ourselves that we will not be happy until we reach our goal. That sentences us to 365 days of unhappiness and dissatisfaction.

Instead, let's fall in love with the process of reaching our goal. We want to do our daily activities with joy. We want to look forward to how we build our business every day. We want to savor the journey. The goal is a milestone, something to celebrate for sure, but it's not our daily reality.

A great way to describe ourselves?

"We are a collection of our habits."

We want to design our life so awesome that we won't need to take a two-week vacation from it. We want to enjoy the process. We want to enjoy our life every day.

Now what?

Does achieving the top 1% in network marketing sentence us to a dull life of boring retirement? Must we sit on a boring beach, staring into the sunset? Must we live in daily frustration looking for our golf ball? Is all that is left for us to do is to take pictures of our food to show to others ... who don't care?

Thankfully ... no.

Remember, the activity that got us to the top 1% is also the activity we would love to do, even if it was free! The old saying is true, "If we love what we do, then we never have to work another day in our lives."

Full-time playing, doing what we love. How good is that?

Our goal shouldn't be to earn enough money so that we can sit around and wait to die. There is much more we can do with our success.

We can celebrate that we are in control of our calendar and schedule. No one else has the power over us to tell us what to do, where to be, and at what time. We truly are our own boss, the boss of our time.

We can reclaim our right to freedom of speech. We don't have to worry that tiny missteps will get us fired.

We don't have to worry about vacations. Vacations from what? Jobs that we hate so bad that we need to vacation from? We don't have that anymore.

We can quit working for money, and worrying about our bank account balance. Instead, we can work for our passions, our family, or to help others.

We can use our success to create opportunities for other people. How good is that? Contribution feels better than receiving.

Just because we reached the top 1% does not mean that our journey is over. Now it is time to live with all the advantages we have by reaching the top 1% in network marketing.

Is our journey worth it? Was mastering the 7 steps a great use of our time? That is for us to decide.

Our future is waiting for us.

More from Big Al Books

See them all at BigAlBooks.com

Mindset Series

Secrets to Mastering Your Mindset
Take Control of Your Network Marketing Career

Breaking the Brain Code
Easy Lessons for Your Network Marketing Career

How to Get Motivated in 60 Seconds
The Secrets to Instant Action

Prospecting and Recruiting Series

Overcoming Objections
Making Network Marketing Rejection-Free

Hooks! The Invisible Sales Superpower
Create Network Marketing Prospects Who Want to Know More

How to Get Appointments Without Rejection
Fill Our Calendars with Network Marketing Prospects

Create Influence
10 Ways to Impress and Guide Others

How to Meet New People Guidebook
Overcome Fear and Connect Now

How to Get Your Prospect's Attention and Keep It!
Magic Phrases for Network Marketing

10 Shortcuts Into Our Prospects' Minds
Get Network Marketing Decisions Fast!

How To Prospect, Sell And Build Your Network Marketing Business With Stories

26 Instant Marketing Ideas To Build Your Network Marketing Business

51 Ways and Places to Sponsor New Distributors
Discover Hot Prospects For Your Network Marketing Business

First Sentences for Network Marketing
How To Quickly Get Prospects On Your Side

Big Al's MLM Sponsoring Magic
How To Build A Network Marketing Team Quickly

Start SuperNetworking!
5 Simple Steps to Creating Your Own Personal Networking Group

Getting Started Series

How to Build Your Network Marketing Business in 15 Minutes a Day

3 Easy Habits For Network Marketing
Automate Your MLM Success

Quick Start Guide for Network Marketing
Get Started FAST, Rejection-FREE!

Four Core Skills Series

How To Get Instant Trust, Belief, Influence and Rapport!
13 Ways To Create Open Minds By Talking To The Subconscious Mind

Ice Breakers!
How To Get Any Prospect To Beg You For A Presentation

Pre-Closing for Network Marketing
"Yes" Decisions Before The Presentation

The Two-Minute Story for Network Marketing
Create the Big-Picture Story That Sticks!

Personality Training Series (The Colors)

The Four Color Personalities for MLM
The Secret Language for Network Marketing

Mini-Scripts for the Four Color Personalities
How to Talk to our Network Marketing Prospects

Why Are My Goals Not Working?
Color Personalities for Network Marketing Success

How To Get Kids To Say Yes!
Using the Secret Four Color Languages to Get Kids to Listen

Presentation and Closing Series

Closing for Network Marketing
Getting Prospects Across The Finish Line

The One-Minute Presentation
Explain Your Network Marketing Business Like A Pro

How to Follow Up With Your Network Marketing Prospects
Turn Not Now Into Right Now!

Retail Sales for Network Marketers
How to Get New Customers for Your MLM Business

Leadership Series

The Complete Three-Book Network Marketing Leadership Series
Series includes: How To Build Network Marketing Leaders Volume One, How To Build Network Marketing Leaders Volume Two, and Motivation. Action. Results.

How To Build Network Marketing Leaders
Volume One: Step-By-Step Creation Of MLM Professionals

How To Build Network Marketing Leaders
Volume Two: Activities And Lessons For MLM Leaders

Motivation. Action. Results.
How Network Marketing Leaders Move Their Teams

What Smart Sponsors Do
Supercharge Our Network Marketing Team

More books...

Why You Need to Start Network Marketing
How to Remove Risk and Have a Better Life

How To Build Your Network Marketing Nutrition Business Fast

How Speakers, Trainers, and Coaches Get More Bookings
12 Ways to Flood Our Calendars with Paid Events

How To Build Your Network Marketing Utilities Business Fast

Getting "Yes" Decisions
What insurance agents and financial advisors can say to clients

Public Speaking Magic
Success and Confidence in the First 20 Seconds

Worthless Sponsor Jokes
Network Marketing Humor

About the Authors

Keith Schreiter has 30+ years of experience in network mar-keting and MLM. He shows network marketers how to use simple systems to build a stable and growing business.

So, do you need more prospects? Do you need your prospects to commit instead of stalling? Want to know how to engage and keep your group active? If these are the types of skills you would like to master, you will enjoy his "how-to" style.

Keith speaks and trains in the U.S., Canada, and Europe.

Tom "Big Al" Schreiter has 50+ years of experience in network marketing and MLM. As the author of the original "Big Al" training books in the late '70s, he has continued to speak in over 80 countries on using the exact words and phrases to get prospects to open up their minds and say "YES."

His passion is marketing ideas, marketing campaigns, and how to speak to the subconscious mind in simplified, practical ways. He is always looking for case studies of incredible marketing campaigns that give usable lessons.

As the author of numerous audio trainings, Tom is a favorite speaker at company conventions and regional events.

Printed in Great Britain
by Amazon

16292003R00061